Heroes for Young Readers

Written by Renee Taft Meloche

Illustrated by Bryan Pollard

Adoniram Judson
Amy Carmichael
Bethany Hamilton
Betty Greene
Brother Andrew
Cameron Townsend
Corrie ten Boom
C. S. Lewis
David Livingstone
Eric Liddell
George Müller

Gladys Aylward
Hudson Taylor
Ida Scudder
Jim Elliot
Jonathan Goforth
Loren Cunningham
Lottie Moon
Mary Slessor
Nate Saint
Nick Vujicic
William Carey

Heroes of History for Young Readers

Written by Renee Taft Meloche

Illustrated by Bryan Pollard

Daniel Boone
Clara Barton
George Washington
George Washington Carver
Meriwether Lewis

Heroes for Young Readers Activity Guides and audio CDs are now available! See the back of this book for more information.

For a free catalog of books and materials contact
YWAM Publishing, P.O. Box 55787, Seattle, WA 98155
1-800-922-2143 www.ywampublishing.com

HEROES FOR YOUNG READERS

NICK VUJICIC

No Limits

Written by Renee Taft Meloche
Illustrated by Bryan Pollard

Nick Vujicic: No Limits   Text © 2014 by Renee Taft Meloche   Illustrations © 2014 by Bryan Pollard
Published by YWAM Publishing, P.O. Box 55787, Seattle, WA 98155   ISBN 978-1-57658-777-5   Printed in China.   All rights reserved.

In beautiful Australia,
	in nineteen eighty-two,
a boy was born who did not look
	the way most babies do.

This baby, Nick, was very cute
	and had the best of care,
but he did not have arms or legs.
	They simply were not there.

He did have one small foot which had
	two toes instead of five,
and as he grew he used this foot
	to hop and swim and dive.

He sometimes tumbled off high chairs,
	off tabletops and beds,
and without arms to catch himself
	he'd hit his chin or head.

Yet Nick would press his forehead up
	against a couch or wall
and inch his body up again
	whenever he would fall.

Just like a gifted gymnast Nick
    could roll and flip and fly.
He loved to test his limits and
    explore new things to try.

Nick's foot could tread and paddle so
    he'd jump in pools and lakes.
He used a power wheelchair
    his foot could operate.

Nick learned to skateboard down steep hills
    and really loved to swim.
As people watched Nick dive and float,
    they were amazed by him.

Young Nick was placed in school when he
        reached kindergarten age.
He used his toes like fingers when
        he drew or turned a page.

Nick's classmates often called him names
        and teased him endlessly.
Nick thought, *They say such hurtful things.*
        Why do they pick on me?

The children also laughed at him,
        which Nick found hard to take.
He wondered, *When God made me, did*
        He make a big mistake?

As Nick kept being kind to kids
no matter what they'd done,
some started being friends with him
and found him lots of fun.

When Nick was six, there was a boy
    named Chucky whom he feared,
a kid with bright orange hair and lots
    of freckles and big ears.

He was a bully who would pick
    on Nick at school each day.
When Chucky dared him to a fight,
    Nick bravely said, "Okay."

Though Nick knew it was wrong to fight
    and could not kick or punch,
he felt he had no choice but to
    agree to fight at lunch.

All morning he felt frightened as
    he thought about his fate.
Nick prayed a teacher would find out
    before it was too late.

But when the lunch bell rang and not
    one teacher said a thing,
Nick moved himself outside and thought,
    This can't be happening.

The other children gathered round.
        Some felt the fight was wrong.
Some brought their lunches. Some took bets.
        Some came to cheer Nick on.

First Chucky spoke and ordered Nick,
        "Get down, get off your chair."
"Then you must get down on your knees,"
        Nick said, "to make it fair."

As Chucky did what he was asked,
        some girls began to cry.
"Don't do it, Nick!" they shouted out.
        "He'll hurt you if you try."

Nick stared at Chucky's smirking face
        and feared what was to come,
but Nick hopped down to fight since he
        had too much pride to run.

Then Chucky hit Nick in the chest
    before he could retreat,
and Nick fell over backward right
    onto the hard concrete.

Nick's classmates huddled over him
    to see if he would rise.
Some girls looked on with great concern.
    Some covered up their eyes.

Nick flipped himself back up again
    and got himself upright,
then took three hops toward Chucky and
    prepared once more to fight.

But Nick was dealt another blow
    and landed on his back.
He felt the wind knocked out of him
    and saw the world go black.

Then Chucky did a victory dance
    and hovered over him.
When Nick woke up he knew the odds
    of beating him were slim.

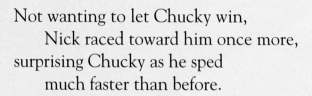

Not wanting to let Chucky win,
    Nick raced toward him once more,
surprising Chucky as he sped
    much faster than before.

As Chucky scooted backward he
    was looking rather scared.
Nick used his foot to launch himself
    up high into the air.

And as Nick flew he took sharp aim
    and what do you suppose?
He used his strong, hard forehead and
    smacked Chucky on the nose.

"Chucky's bleeding!" one girl yelled.
    The children stood there stunned,
since Nick, who could not kick or punch,
    now looked like he had won.

As Chucky sat there on the ground
    and held his nose and cried,
Nick thought he'd feel so glad to win
    yet just felt bad inside.

Some kids began to cheer as Nick
    asked Chucky, "You all right?"
As Chucky stood he hid his face
    and scurried out of sight.

Nick never, ever had to fear
    his bully after that,
for Chucky left the school that day
    and never did come back.

Though Nick was glad he'd bravely faced
    his bully squarely on,
he never fought again because
    it felt so very wrong.

When Nick was twelve he left his land—
    the land of kangaroos—
and moved to California where
    there were no kids he knew.

Since Nick had left his friends behind,
    he felt a growing fear.
He wondered as he started school,
    Will they accept me here?

A boy named Andrew picked on Nick.
    His words were very cruel.
As others too made fun of him,
    Nick started dreading school.

"Nick has a tire that is flat,"
    one kid would say in jest.
"Let's use Nick as a doorstop then,"
    another would suggest.

Nick tried avoiding Andrew since
    his words hurt Nick the most.
Nick felt so scared his heart beat fast
    whenever he was close.

Some older kids thought Andrew should
      be shaken up a bit,
and volunteered to beat him up
      so he'd be nice to Nick.

Nick hoped there was a better way
      to make the teasing stop.
He'd speak to Andrew, praying that
      they'd have a peaceful talk.

The next time Nick was teased by him,
      instead of shrinking back,
Nick boldly went right up and asked,
      "Why are you saying that?"

"It hurts me when you say those things,"
      and Andrew looked surprised.
"I only meant it as a joke.
      I'm sorry," he replied.

Nick said, "I do forgive you," since
      he seemed to feel quite bad,
and after that the teasing stopped,
      which made Nick very glad.

Returning to Australia,
    Nick struggled once again
as people called him hurtful names
    like "freak" and "alien."

Nick prayed, "Creator God, please grow
    some arms and legs for me,
so I can show this miracle
    for all the world to see."

Nick's parents often said that God
had special plans for him,
but Nick was sad and angry when
he did not grow one limb.

Yet slowly Nick accepted what
he could and could not do.
He'd do his best with what he had
and would be grateful too.

At lunchtime Nick had often hid
    while classmates were at play,
but he became more friendly now
    and did not shy away.

In high school Nick spoke openly
    as he felt less afraid.
He shared how he could now accept
    the way that he was made.

He said, "We don't all look alike.
    We all have different hair.
We might be slow, we might be fast,
    or use a wheelchair."

"Not everyone is smart at math
    or great at playing sports,
and no two faces are the same.
    We might be tall or short."

"Our God has made us beautiful
in different ways," Nick said,
which helped the kids be kind to those
they once had teased instead.

Nick spoke to one large group of teens
    and noticed in surprise
that half of them who sat there had
    big teardrops in their eyes.

One girl began to sob out loud
    as tears rolled down her cheeks.
She raised her head, then raised her hand
    and stood up from her seat.

She went to Nick, gave him a hug,
then whispered in his ear,
"No one has said I'm beautiful
until you told me here."

Nick finished school, then studied at
a university.
Today he's on the radio
and also on TV.

He lives in California with
his son and lovely wife.
He speaks around the world and shares
true stories from his life.

Nick's differences don't hold him back
    from having lots of fun.
He surfs big waves, goes snorkeling,
    rides horses and plays drums.

Nick skydives and plays soccer too.
    He bounces balls and types.
He loves to paint and act and sing
    and publish books he writes.

Though some things are much easier
    for those with feet and hands,
there's nothing that will stop Nick from
    the full life God has planned.

Nick's learned that we should not give up
because he knows it's true:
with God there are no limits to
the things that we can do.

Christian Heroes: Then & Now

by Janet & Geoff Benge

Adoniram Judson: Bound for Burma
Amy Carmichael: Rescuer of Precious Gems
Betty Greene: Wings to Serve
Brother Andrew: God's Secret Agent
Cameron Townsend: Good News in Every Language
Clarence Jones: Mr. Radio
Corrie ten Boom: Keeper of the Angels' Den
Count Zinzendorf: Firstfruit
C. S. Lewis: Master Storyteller
C. T. Studd: No Retreat
David Bussau: Facing the World Head-on
David Livingstone: Africa's Trailblazer
Dietrich Bonhoeffer: In the Midst of Wickedness
D. L. Moody: Bringing Souls to Christ
Elisabeth Elliot: Joyful Surrender
Eric Liddell: Something Greater Than Gold
Florence Young: Mission Accomplished
Francis Asbury: Circuit Rider
George Müller: The Guardian of Bristol's Orphans
Gladys Aylward: The Adventure of a Lifetime
Hudson Taylor: Deep in the Heart of China
Ida Scudder: Healing Bodies, Touching Hearts
Isobel Kuhn: On the Roof of the World
Jacob DeShazer: Forgive Your Enemies
Jim Elliot: One Great Purpose
John Wesley: The World His Parish
John Williams: Messenger of Peace
Jonathan Goforth: An Open Door in China
Lillian Trasher: The Greatest Wonder in Egypt
Loren Cunningham: Into All the World
Lottie Moon: Giving Her All for China
Mary Slessor: Forward into Calabar
Nate Saint: On a Wing and a Prayer
Paul Brand: Helping Hands
Rachel Saint: A Star in the Jungle
Rowland Bingham: Into Africa's Interior
Samuel Zwemer: The Burden of Arabia
Sundar Singh: Footprints Over the Mountains
Wilfred Grenfell: Fisher of Men
William Booth: Soup, Soap, and Salvation
William Carey: Obliged to Go

Heroes for Young Readers and Heroes of History for Young Readers are based on the Christian Heroes: Then & Now and Heroes of History biographies by Janet & Geoff Benge. Don't miss out on these exciting, true adventures for ages 10 and up!

Heroes of History
by Janet & Geoff Benge

Abraham Lincoln: A New Birth of Freedom
Alan Shepard: Higher and Faster
Benjamin Franklin: Live Wire
Captain John Smith: A Foothold in the New World
Christopher Columbus: Across the Ocean Sea
Clara Barton: Courage under Fire
Daniel Boone: Frontiersman
Davy Crockett: Ever Westward
Douglas MacArthur: What Greater Honor
George Washington Carver: From Slave to Scientist
George Washington: True Patriot
Harriet Tubman: Freedombound
John Adams: Independence Forever
Laura Ingalls Wilder: A Storybook Life
Meriwether Lewis: Off the Edge of the Map
Milton Hershey: More Than Chocolate
Orville Wright: The Flyer
Ronald Reagan: Destiny at His Side
Theodore Roosevelt: An American Original
Thomas Edison: Inspiration and Hard Work
William Penn: Liberty and Justice for All

...and more coming soon. Unit Study Curriculum Guides are also available.

Heroes for Young Readers Activity Guides
Educational and Character-Building Lessons for Children
by Renee Taft Meloche

Heroes for Young Readers Activity Guide for Books 1–4
Gladys Aylward, Eric Liddell, Nate Saint, George Müller

Heroes for Young Readers Activity Guide for Books 5–8
Amy Carmichael, Corrie ten Boom, Mary Slessor, William Carey

Heroes for Young Readers Activity Guide for Books 9–12
Betty Greene, David Livingstone, Adoniram Judson, Hudson Taylor

Heroes for Young Readers Activity Guide for Books 13–16
Jim Elliot, Cameron Townsend, Jonathan Goforth, Lottie Moon

Heroes of History for Young Readers Activity Guide for Books 1–4
George Washington Carver, Meriwether Lewis, George Washington, Clara Barton

Designed to accompany the vibrant Heroes for Young Readers books, these fun-filled Activity Guides lead young children through a variety of character-building and educational activities. Pick and choose from the activities or follow the included thirteen-week syllabus. An audio CD with book readings, songs, and fun activity tracks is available for each Activity Guide.

For a free catalog of books and materials contact
YWAM Publishing, P.O. Box 55787, Seattle, WA 98155
1-800-922-2143 www.ywampublishing.com